Spun Out on Shame? Reclaim Your Sanity

"You were Meant for More" Series

Tamara J. Buchan
Lindsey D. Osborne

RECLAIM
MINISTRIES

SANTA ROSA
CALIFORNIA

ISBN-13: 978-1507650400
ISBN-10: 150765040X

Quoted Scripture:
Quoted Scripture:
Scripture quotations marked NRSV are taken from the New Revised Standard Version Bible, copyright 1989, Division of Christian Education of the National Council of the Churches of Christ in the United States of America. Used by permission. All rights reserved.

Quoted Scripture from BibleGateway.com:
Scripture quotations marked NIV are taken from the HOLY BIBLE, NEW INTERNA-TIONAL VERSION®. NIV®. Copyright © 1973, 1978, 1984, 2011 by Biblica, Inc.™ Used by permission. All rights reserved worldwide.

Scripture quotations marked NLT are taken from the Holy Bible. New Living Translation copyright© 1996, 2004, 2007 by Tyndale House Foundation. Used by permission of Tyndale House Publishers, Inc. Carol Stream, Illinois 60188. All rights reserved.

Scripture quotations marked NASB are taken from the New American Standard Bible, © 1960, 1962, 1963, 1968, 1971, 1972, 1973, 1975, 1977, 1995 by The Lockman Foundation. Used by permission.

Cover Art and Design: Andrew and Brenda Emmert.
Graphic Design: Anne Thompson, Ebookannie, www.ebookannie.com.

I prayed to the Lord, and he answered me.

He freed me from all my fears.

Those who look to him for help will be radiant with joy;

No shadow of SHAME will darken their faces.

In my desperation I prayed, and the Lord listened;

He saved me from all my troubles.

Psalm 34:4-6

Dedication

This book is Dedicated to Everyone
who has ever Experienced the Great Theft of Shame.

Our Dream is for the World to be a **"Shame-Free"** zone!

It starts with each one of us Reclaiming our True Identity:
as a Beloved Child who Belongs
in God's Great Big Family,
rather than as a Captive,
Isolated within the Prison of Shame.

TABLE OF CONTENTS

Foreword

As beautiful as this world is, as often as life brings us beauty, love and joy, most of us are all-too familiar with fear, loss and shame. And while fear can affect our outlook and loss can upset our stability, shame infects our identity.

Authors Tamara Buchan and Lindsey Osborne have written a book together that offers keen analysis and personal insights into the lies and thievery of shame. *Spun out on Shame? Reclaim Your Sanity* helps us think about our own struggles with shame and identity and offers practical steps we can take to find our true identity.

Guilt and shame are issues we all deal with, whether knowingly or unknowingly. Guilt usually requires some sort of amend, but if we're willing to pursue it, resolution can happen. Shame, on the other hand, leaves a stain. Shame becomes a penetrating indictment, one that is not easily dismissed.

Guilt causes the occasional or recurring awareness of "I have done something wrong," but shame afflicts us with the abiding accusation that "there is something wrong with me."

The most startling story of suffering in human history is that of Jesus of Nazareth. He voluntarily laid aside his Divine Dignity and Eternal Power to forever bind his Godly nature with our human nature, so that he could live among us and offer himself to us. He made this stunning, redemptive move to restore relational unity between the Holy and Loving God and his broken and rebellious children. Our guilt made us distant; our shame made us estranged. Invading our shame-filled shadows, Jesus made the costly offering to bring us home.

Hebrews 2 offers an astounding truth about Jesus, redemption and our ongoing struggle with shame. The writer says that, as Jesus has taken on our human nature for eternity and lived among us, he shares in our suffering and is never ashamed to call us brothers and sisters.

If he is not ashamed of us, who are we to shame ourselves? Or each other?

Tamara Buchan and Lindsey Osborne help us confront our own traps with shame and lead us on the road to the holistic freedom Jesus made possible for each of us.

T.C. Ryan
The Shame No More Project
Phone: 913-226-5217
Email: tcryanone@gmail.com
Facebook: T. C. Ryan
Twitter: @tcryanone

Shame doesn't simply affect our identity, it INFECTS our identity.

Shame robs us of the life we were intended to live, and keeps us separated from God and one another. It seeps out into every part of our lives; infecting key relationships, our ability to step into our full potential, and even our bodily health.

We believe shame is on God's mind in this season and God wants to see it eradicated – totally! He is giving courageous people the ability to confront it head-on and to lock it within the same prison where we've been held captive.

We can be free—and let God's love and our identity as beloved children in his family become our true home.

If you don't believe that shame is on God's mind, think again. Scripture contains **358** references to shame. Much of it is *God **moving to shame our enemies*** because of his great love for us.

It's like a Dad, defending his daughter on the playground because the bully has been taunting her and making her life miserable.

Shame is our enemy.

It torments us and makes our life miserable.

Our Dad moves on our behalf to put shame to death.

Consider this Scripture in Psalm 34:4-6:

> I prayed to the Lord, and he answered me. He freed me from all my fears.
>
> Those who look to him for help will be radiant with

joy;

No shadow of SHAME will darken their face

In my desperation I prayed, and the Lord listened

He saved me from all my troubles.

The differences are tangible: connection with the Lord, which brings answered prayers, freedom from fear, joy instead of desperation, and relief from constant trouble.

A life free from shame – are you ready for the journey?

Fasten your seatbelt: it's time to live the adventure!

P.S. We've developed a very practical tool for exchanging your *Shame Stealers Replaced by Truth Sealers* located in the **Appendix** so that you can get started on your journey to freedom!

 Before reading the Introduction, watch the video: *Spun out on Shame Introduction*. Go to, http://www. reclaimidentity.org/spun-out-on-shame-reclaim-your-sanity.html or scan the QR Code.

Introduction

Shame.

We've all heard the expression, "Shame on you."

Perhaps we heard it daily growing up. Maybe it's left an indelible imprint upon us. Perhaps so much that no matter how many times we try to push it back into the dark corner of our mind, it manages to pop out and remind us over and over, "You aren't good enough. You aren't worthy to be happy, to be loved, or to succeed."

Maybe you've dealt with shame.

You want to be free.

Perhaps you've gone to counseling and gotten clear about why you experience shame, and your head understands the "shame on you" messages don't belong.

But what about your heart – does it know this, too?

- Shame tries to tell us we don't belong; we were meant to feel alone and lonely.

- Shame lies to us, telling us we can't succeed; our dreams were meant to be buried and forgotten – forever.

- Shame wraps around us like armor, keeping us from experiencing friendship and intimacy with others, telling us over and over, its better this way; then they will never know what a screw-up we are.

Here's the reality for all of us.

Shame steals.

It robbed the first people in the Garden of Eden, Adam and Eve, and it's robbed everyone ever created, including you.

Including me. None of us have escaped it completely.

Shame lies.

And now it's time to destroy shame forever in our lives.

Come with me on this journey, and together we can discover the root of our shame and dig it out, setting the landscapes of our lives onto a solid foundation of identity as the beloved, unconditionally accepted, celebrated, kids of our Creator: our Heavenly Father.

CHAPTER 1

THE LIFE WE WERE MEANT TO LIVE

The lyrics of a popular 2014 pop song highlight the enlightenment we gain through opposites.

In *"Let Her Go,"* the band Passenger sang,

Well you only need the light when it's burning low

Only miss the sun when it starts to snow

Only know you love her when you let her go

Only know you've been high when you're feeling low

Only hate the road when you're missin' home

Only know you love her when you let her go...

And you let her go.

Listen to *Let Her Go,* by Passenger. Go to, https://www.youtube.com/watch?v=RBumgq5yVrA or scan the QR Code.

Indeed, we often don't know fully what we have, feel, or experience, unless we can also know the opposite.

We cannot know the full and dreadful effects of shame on our lives without experiencing the life we were designed to live. Shame sent us into a downward spiral of chaos, leaving us spun out, tired, and broken. Instead, **we were supposed to settle in peace**- in the astounding home our Creator made for us.

So let's go there, as we explore what God meant for us to experience.

The Bible paints an amazing picture of the Garden of Eden. The word, *"eden"* means paradise.

And **indeed it was a paradise:**

> All the trees, plants, flowers and bushes flourished. Animals ran wild, but all got along.

> Birds soared overhead and sang their beautiful songs. Rivers flowed freely and abundantly.

> Creation was in perfect synergy. Nothing ever died; everything continued to prosper and multiply.

Not only was creation moving like a magnificent symphony with its instruments in seamless harmony, *life between Adam and Eve was our greatest dream* for relationships come true. It went beyond it, actually, because once shame entered the Garden, we can't fully imagine it.

We've experienced too much relational brokenness.

But without a vision our dreams die, so let's try to envision what our lives and relationships were meant to be; as God originally designed them.

Adam had a great position, and experienced amazing success in his work. As manager of the Garden, he was to oversee it, tend it, and creatively name the livestock, birds and wild animals.

However, Adam was lonely doing this work alone. He longed for a partner to work alongside him. He knew something was wrong, but he couldn't quite name his deep yearning.

But God knew.

He put Adam into a deep sleep (the first surgery!), and took a rib from him. He created a woman from the rib and brought her to Adam.

Listen to what Adam exclaimed:

"Wow, at last! This one is bone from my bone, and flesh from my flesh. She is called 'woman' because she was taken from man."

Adam knew Eve, his wife, fully completed him.

His longing for companionship and intimacy was fulfilled. **They moved as one—sexually, emotionally and spiritually.** They worked together in the Garden; watching everything they named and touched thrive.

Nothing separated them. Nothing.

They kept no secrets from one another.

They didn't have even an ounce of embarrassment about their bodies.

They had no fears or scars from past broken relationships.

- They only knew love.
- They only knew security.
- They only knew trust.
- They only knew honor.

- They only knew intimacy.

Life in the Garden was every human's dream come true.

Garden life is the life we were created to live.

Reflect

1. *Look back*: What are some of your best memories? When have you experienced high heights?

2. *Take inventory*: Currently, does your life look like you thought it would when you were setting out as an adult? Are you living a life that feels like the "life we are created to live"?

3. *Dream forward*: If you could change three things about how your life feels right now, what would they be?

DO something!

Brainstorm perfect combinations.

What synergistic pairs do you enjoy? Chocolate and mint? Peanut butter and jelly? Wine and chocolate? Sunday afternoons and football? Saturday mornings and long runs?

When two things relate in perfect harmony, the effect is often great pleasure. Think of how well-connected Adam and Eve were with each other and with God. This week, enjoy some combinations that you can get your hands on, and consider what it would be like to be in the perfect relationship.

CHAPTER 2

OUR TRUE FATHER

Adam and Eve experienced heaven on earth in their relationship, because their father was the Creator of the Garden and the whole universe.

He created them for relationships – yes, with one another, but even more with himself.

For more on relationship, see *A Shared Life Together: Relationship Reclaimed*. Go to http://www.reclaimidentity.org/a-shared-life-together-relationship-reclaimed.html or scan the QR Code.

Read Chapter 1 in *Identity Crisis: Reclaim the True You, Our True Purpose*. Go to http://www.reclaimidentity.org/chapter-1-our-true-purpose.html or scan the QR Code.

Imagine this: we were created for relationship with the Creator of the entire Universe who knows and cares about every part of our lives.

He dreamed of a home for his kids, which include the elements of his home in heaven: peace, joy, play, creativity, intimacy, fulfilling work, rest, protection, and community.

He not only created a heavenly home for Adam and Eve, and all his other kids, he deposited his DNA within us.

Genesis 1:27 tells us:

> "So God created humanity in his image. In the image of God he created them; male and female he created them."

Every person who has ever lived has God's DNA within them.

- They were created to look like their heavenly father.

- They carry his heart and his character.

- They are given heavenly creativity, to fulfill their "garden" appointment.

Hey, wait – this isn't just for the "other people over there."

It's meant for you too!

- You were created in God's image.

- You carry his DNA within you, too.

Living with the divine image in us means that we can reclaim our human capacity for goodness. We were not created broken, lost, or trapped in sin. Instead, we were created with the capacity for individual freedom, reason, spiritual perception, personal uniqueness, community, mystery and life.

We were meant to live deeply connected to God and vitally connected to the natural world, with both the ability and the impetus to do good work, with and for others.

You are his beloved child.

You are meant to live in a garden where everything thrives, and nothing ever dies.

Reflect:

1. *Look back:* What parts of you look the most like your parents? Even if you aren't their biological child, what about your behavior connects you to the people with whom you grew up?

2. *Take inventory:* Reflect on what it means to be created in God's image. What does it mean to be created good, whole, and for relationship? Does this thinking challenge or confirm beliefs you hold about humanity?

3. *Dream forward:* Think about someone else you know who doesn't live feeling loved. How can you retell these truths in a way that would encourage them to know they are good and that God loves them deeply?

DO Something:

Rephrase, retell, and live out the truth of this chapter. Share the story with someone else.

www.ReclaimIdentity.org

CHAPTER 3

THE "NAKED" TRUTH

Have you ever heard people call the Bible boring? There was a time when I thought the same thing. But now, I see that it has all of the elements of a great story. In some passages, the truth is provocative, other times, it's lying beneath the surface, waiting for us to stop, to dig deeper and to dive in.

Watch video: *The Naked Truth*. Go to http://www.reclaimidentity.org/a-shared-life-together-relationship-reclaimed.html or scan the QR Code. (If unable to view, read the video script at the end of the book, p. 75)

Here is one example. The second chapter of Genesis ends with the stunning declaration:

"Adam and Eve were both naked and they felt no shame."

Interesting.

Adam and Eve were naked, and unashamed.

What about us today? In my experience, there aren't many places I am naked and unashamed.

Think *gym showers* in those awkward middle school years.

My birthday is in the middle of August, so when I began junior high, I was barely 12. I was a really small child, so when most of my friends began to develop, I was still flat-chested. So board-like in fact, one embarrassing afternoon my Mom took me to buy a bra (per my request to be like my friends) and the store couldn't find one small enough for me.

Consequently, I spent the whole summer before junior high dreading gym class and the horrifying reality that I would have to be naked in front of my peers. I knew my body didn't measure up.

Despite the skin we see splattered on screens all around us, no one wants to be physically naked in front of unsafe people. For most of us, being naked emotionally is even scarier.

How much energy do you expend trying to re-create and sustain your personality, in order to make sure that no one knows the real you?

Doubt rattles oppressively around in our heads: "If they really knew _____ about me, then they would... (leave, laugh, abuse, exploit, discard, or avoid) me." How do you fill in the blanks??

Are you wearing emotional clothing to disguise the real you?

Today, we feel a connection between nakedness and shame. In the garden, between Adam and Eve, there was also nakedness – physically, yes, but of even greater importance, there was emotional and spiritual nakedness. All this nakedness, and yet they didn't have any idea about shame.

For Adam and Eve, shame wasn't in their vocabulary because in their world, shame simply didn't exist.

Reflect:

1. *Look back:* What are some of the earliest insecurities you carried? Did you impose them upon yourself or come under them because of someone else's actions?

2. *Take inventory:* What are the biggest insecurities you carry today? Are you hiding the real you? Deep down, do people really get to see the true you?

3. *Dream forward:* What is one thing you hide that you'd love to get out in the open?

Do Something:

Be naked. This week, in the shower, take inventory. Accept your body as the gift, home, tool that it is. As the water washes over you, think about how raw and vulnerable you are when you're naked. Think about your emotional and spiritual vulnerability. Are you ever truly naked?

CHAPTER 4

THE ULTIMATE SEDUCTION

Adam and Eve had complete freedom in the garden. They had their father's full permission and instruction to create, to play, and to eat daily from the *Tree of Life*. As long as they ate from the *Tree of Life*, they would experience the amazing life their Father designed for them. Their bodies would be fed, their creativity would expand, their spirits would be fully alive, and their relationships with God, their relationships with one another, and creation as a whole would thrive.

In the garden, Adam and Eve had complete freedom.

They had just one boundary: *not to eat from the **Tree of the Knowledge of Good and Evil**.*

Just as nakedness and shame are polar opposites, the *Tree of Life* and the *Tree of the Knowledge of Good and Evil* are extreme opposites.

One brings life, and the other death.

Here's what their heavenly father said to them:

> "You may eat freely from the fruit of every tree in the garden, except the *Tree of the Knowledge of Good and Evil*. If you eat its fruit, you are sure to die." Genesis 2:15

Of course, they had no idea about death. It had never happened in the garden. For a while, life was glorious.

- Adam and Eve experienced the full intimacy they were created to live.

- They experienced life with their father as he intended: free, open, fulfilling.

- Their vocation thrilled and fed them.

- Their bodies were healthy, their spirits nurtured, and finances overflowing.

As in every good story, an antagonist must exist.

The garden's antagonist was the sly and slimy serpent.

However, Adam and Eve did not realize he was to play the evil part. They saw only his outward colors, not his true heart.

His agenda and character remained hidden.

He was a shrewd and patient serpent, determining to talk to Eve when she was alone, without Adam, so that she would be more vulnerable to his deceitful scheme.

And so, **one day the serpent saw his opportunity for seduction.**

It was the day that would forever change Eve's life.

He came up to her, casually asking, "Did God *really* say you must not eat from any tree of the garden?"

Eve innocently answered, "Of course not, silly. We can eat from any tree in the garden, except the *Tree of the Knowledge of Good and Evil*. If we eat from that tree, or even touch it, we will die."

The serpent knew too much than to confront Eve head-on with a lie; so he wrapped his lie in truth. He had his facts straight… almost. God **did** say not to eat from the *Tree of the Knowledge of Good and Evil,* but only after he had offered everything else.

Coded into the serpents question was the bigger question, "Is God holding out on you?"

Is God holding out on *you*?

Hmm. Have you ever considered that?

Adam and Eve had abundance, and they had a choice. We have the same.

God freely gives, and we get to respond. We can choose to gratefully accept the gifts and give thanks, or to miss out on the true gifts because of pride, ingratitude or fear.

The serpent's next coded lie: **"You won't die!** God knows your eyes will be opened as soon as you eat it and you will become like him, knowing both good and evil."

Can you find the lies here?

The first is obvious, the second is hidden.

> Eating from the *Tree of the Knowledge of Good and Evil* does kill – and they will die.

The second lie is "and you will become like him."

> They already were like God.

They were his kids and every child carries their parent's DNA.

They were made in his image.

They had his character and his creativity.

Even more insidious is the lie that God is withholding from them—that he isn't giving them all the benefits that come with being his kids.

Eve begins to listen. She is eager; she wants to experience everything, with nothing held back.

The *seduction* continues.

Eve begins to move toward the tree, and as she does, her husband comes to join her.

- She looks intently.
- She sees the tree is beautiful to look upon.
- She is enticed by how delicious its fruit appears.

Her appetite cries out to be fed. Suddenly, all the resources in the garden, including *The Tree of Life*, don't seem to be enough.

Even greater, Eve wanted the wisdom she believed she would gain by eating the fruit. After all, God had access to something she didn't have: the knowledge of evil.

In that moment, Eve developed a **"not enough" mentality.**

This is a danger point.

The "not enough" mentality tempts us to believe we can fill ourselves. It takes us away from relationship with our heavenly father.

It was dangerous for Eve, because she reached out her hand, put it on the fruit and pulled it from the tree. Sadly, the very one, Adam, who was given the mandate to protect her, stood idly by and watched her do it. In fact, he even took a piece of fruit from Eve and ate it with her.

The serpent smiled. He had completed his shrewd, patient seduction.

Life was never the same in the garden. It isn't the same today.

Oh, the grief and devastation of it all.

Reflect:

1. *Look back*: Have you heard or read these commands to Adam and Eve before? Is your first response to think God is uptight, controlling, or restrictive?

2. *Take inventory*: What limits do you live by? Think speed limits, diets, stopping work and going to bed at night, not drinking and driving, etc. What purpose do these limits serve? Why choose to obey them?

3. *Dream forward:* Do God's restraints for us, such as these directives to Adam and Eve, or even the Ten Commandments, bring you security or make you feel constricted? Why do you think that is?

DO Something:

If we believe God is holding out on us, we view God through a restrictive and foggy filter. Lies about God's character continue to be lodged in our direction. As you practice a limit this week-driving your car the speed limit, not eating dessert, letting go of a list of to-dos to pay better attention to a person, or whatever you have, pay attention to the life that grows out of that limit. Does some restriction actually lead to greater freedom?

www.ReclaimIdentity.org

CHAPTER 5

SEDUCTION'S OUTCOME: SHAME

I used to think if I were Eve, I would have made a different choice. But I know better now. I have been tempted into too many areas where suddenly the "temptation" standing before me seemed much greater than my heavenly father; who, after all, is busy in heaven doing his heavenly thing.

A lie can sometimes look bigger than love.

Broken by temptation, constantly lusting for something real and whole, we fill in the blanks with something temporary we believe will satisfy us.

Read *Five Stages of Identity: Success Reclaimed.* Go to http://www.reclaimidentity.org/five-stages-of-identity-success-reclaimed.html or scan the QR Code.

Name it... we've used it all as a balm to soothe the senses, as a distraction to keep the dark at bay, or as a band-aid to cover up and minimally protect the pain for a period of time.

Eventually, we always come to the realization of what we've done through our pursuit of pleasure. Our immediate response is shame; the tangled web of shame catches us in its net and holds us captive.

Right now, my own battle of temptation is food. I eat a healthy diet, but in those quiet moments at night, *my pantry beckons me seductively.*

If I walk into it, it's as if all the delicious food is crying out, **"Pick me. Pick me."**

On strong days, I walk out, realizing what's happening. But, all too often, I do pick one, and possibly another, and maybe even another. My stomach tells me its satisfied but in the morning, I wake up with. . . you know it: **SHAME!**

Regret, shame's younger sister, sleeps with me.

Even as I sit here, I don't want to expose this to you. I'd rather keep it a secret and make you think that I am writing this book from the place of having it all together. After all, if I do have it all together, you will listen to what I have to say, right?

IMPOSSIBLE!

None of us has it all together.

And yet, all too often we betray our conscience, and believe a lie – we think everyone else has it together; **I am the only screw-up in the midst.**

Here's the reality.

- This lie keeps us hidden.

- It keeps us isolated.

- It keeps us going to the _____(fill in the blank) that we believe will satisfy us.

Remember Genesis 2:25? We explored the glory of this reality: "Now the man and his wife were both **naked and they felt no shame.**"

In seven short verses, everything has dramatically shifted.

Genesis 3:7: "At that moment their eyes were opened, and they suddenly **felt shame at their nakedness.**"

That which before was purity and innocence and complete trust has now been denigrated to **SHAME.**

Adam and Eve's trust and complete security in their relationship with God and with one another has been shattered into a million pieces.

Horrifically embarrassed over their nakedness, they run to hide and to cover themselves. Hunched over behind a bush, they invent fashion. There, in hiddenness, they struggle to craft meager clothes out of fig leaves.

I wonder what they were thinking as they sewed their first clothes.

- Did they wonder if they would ever be free to reveal their nakedness with delight again?
- Did they wonder if they would ever feel safe in one another's arms again?
- Did they wonder if they would ever again be able to share their deepest dreams?

Ultimately, at the moment of reaching out for the forbidden fruit, they broke the complete trust they had in one another and in their heavenly father.

Everything in the universe shifted in that moment.

Let's sit with that for a moment. We dared to dream about what life could be like in the garden for us. We dabbled in imagining abundance. We started to believe we could put down the shield we wield for protection against disappointment.

Now, however, we attempt to not just hold up the shield but to invest in the armor that would surround our whole body from the arrows that come at us all day long, speaking the words that keep us in our place: "Who are you to believe that you could be. . .

- Known?

- Or celebrated?

- Or valued?

- Or successful?

- Or loved?"

No matter how strong the armor, our heart is always vulnerable and exposed. And in those quiet moments, **our heart screams out for its true home, the garden.** For that is where we were created to live.

Reflect:

1. *Look back:* What have been some of your favorite articles of clothing? On a deeper note, what covers do you "wear" emotionally to hide deeper feelings?

2. *Take inventory:* Keep thinking about what you currently bury. What is hiding underneath the outward, visible parts of your life? Have you lost the ability to dream towards wholeness or renewed safety, freedom from pain, or relational reconciliation? Are there places where you've lost all hope?

3. *Dream forward:* What shame do you want to get rid of? What freedom would fill in the empty spot left by scooped-out shame?

DO Something:

Check out Tom Ryan's website and blog at http:// tc-ryan.com or scan the QR Code. Find a support group that will allow you to come naked into their healing process. Find a friend who will hear your story – all the ugly, scary parts of it – and hold it carefully, helping you find a way to lay it down and walk away.

Watch the videos by T.C. Ryan or scan the QR Codes

Part 1, https://www.youtube.com/watch?v=Ib8y2 CGF3oI&feature=youtu.be

Part 2, https://www.youtube.com/watch?v=HEgl UnK_8HU&feature=youtu.be

www.ReclaimIdentity.org

CHAPTER 6

SHAME'S DOWNWARD SPIRAL

I remember the first time I heard *Brené Brown's Ted Talks*. I thought to myself, "Her research has origin in Genesis 3. The same shame effects Brené discovered in her eight years of research are listed in the Bible's beginning."

Watch the video: *Listening to Shame.* Go to https:// www.youtube.com/watch?v=psN1DORYYV0 or scan the QR Code.

I don't think it's an accident so many people are captivated by her discussion on shame and vulnerability. I think our heavenly father is just plain weary of the suffering we experience because of shame.

He sent Jesus, his son, who lived in love and freedom, to reveal how shame robs us, kills us, and destroys relationships. With each other and with him. Digging deeply into the great theft Adam and Eve experienced, we may see our own lives reflected in theirs.

Read Genesis 3:7-19 (the text is below) once all the way through, *putting yourself in the garden*, and discovering the dramatic shift that you are experiencing, now that you have discovered the reality of "shame," the very exposure which your Heavenly Father sought to protect you from ever experiencing.

Genesis 3:7-19

> At that moment their eyes were opened, and they suddenly felt shame at their nakedness. So they sewed fig leaves together to cover themselves. When they heard the sound of GOD strolling in the garden in the evening breeze, the Man and his Wife hid in the trees of the garden, hid from GOD.

GOD called to the Man: "Where are you?"

> He said, "I heard you in the garden and I was afraid because I was naked. And I hid."

> GOD said, "Who told you were naked? Did you eat from that tree I told you not to eat from?"

> The Man said, "The Woman you gave me as a companion, she gave me fruit from the tree, and, yes, I ate it."

GOD said to the Woman, "What is this that you've done?"

> "The serpent seduced me," she said, "and I ate."

GOD told the serpent:

> "Because you've done this, you're cursed, cursed beyond all cattle and wild animals, cursed to slink on your belly and eat dirt all your life. I'm declaring war between you and the Woman, between your offspring and hers. He'll wound your head, you'll wound his heel."

He told the Woman:

> "I'll multiply your pains in childbirth; you'll give birth to your babies in pain. You'll want to please your husband, but he'll lord it over you."

He told the Man:

> "Because you listened to your wife and ate from the tree that I commanded you not to eat from, 'Don't eat from this tree,' the very ground is cursed because of you; getting food from the ground
>
> Will be as painful as having babies is for your wife; you'll be working in pain all your life long. The ground will sprout thorns and weeds, you'll get your food the hard way, planting and tilling and harvesting, sweating in the fields from dawn to dusk, until you return to that ground yourself, dead and buried; you started out as dirt, you'll end up dirt."

Adam and Eve, while originally living in peaceful, abundant perfection, **became spun out on shame**.

Shame's downward spiral is one that wreaks relational division, personal implosion, and communal unrest.

The entry point is **shame**. Everything else flows from it.

The garden story illustrates shame's destructive path. The spiral of shame leaves a long checklist of damages. Adam and Eve realized with dismay that they were naked and ran to hide. Just moments before, they had been **innocent and free,** now they find themselves hiding behind a bush, seeking to wear its fruit. They are ashamed of their choice, dreading the moment their father comes seeking them in the garden. They suddenly believe they aren't worthy of his love.

CHECKLIST: Shame brings loss of vulnerability.

> God comes to them, as he did every afternoon, calling out, "Adam, where are you?"
>
> Adam sheepishly responds, "I was **afraid**, so I **hid.**

CHECKLIST: Shame brings loss of vulnerability, **and fear and hiding.**

Did you realize shame has the same physical results as trauma?

Shame puts us into a fight or flight mode: it causes our brain to go into an emotional response that can cause us to break out into a sweat, our hands to tingle, our minds to go blank, our hearts to beat rapidly, our bodies to faint, and our skin break out in a cold sweat.

Fear keeps us bound, afraid to move forward toward our dreams.

Hiding keeps us isolated, afraid to move toward the people we long to know more intimately.

God asks Adam, giving him the chance to step up and take responsibility for his choice, "Who told you were naked?"

Skirting around personal responsibility, Adam **blames** his wife. "It was that woman you gave me. She gave me the fruit, so I ate it."

Did you hear what he said? *"That woman you gave me."*

Yesterday Adam was in complete oneness with his wife; the ecstasy of their relationship *satisfied* his every longing.

Today, he is calling her "that woman you gave me." He is not only **blaming his wife,** he is **blaming God** for giving her to him.

Not only is he blaming God for creating Eve, Adam **rejects** her by letting the wall of shame come crashing down between them.

CHECKLIST: Shame brings loss of vulnerability, fear and hiding, **blame and rejection.**

The definition of blame is: "to hold responsible, to find fault with, to place responsibility for (something); censure, condemnation."

Interestingly, the root of the word blame comes from **blasphemy**, which means "a contemptuous or profane act, utterance, or writing against God or a sacred entity, or the act of claiming for oneself the attributes and rights of God."

The reality is using blame to *avert responsibility,* mostly away from oneself and in condemnation towards another.

Blame shifting never brings health; it always causes harm. Blame's effects are far reaching: into our relationships, our vocations, our culture, our government – the list continues.

Nothing ever changes for the better when blame is involved.

We all know rejection. It hits us hard and makes us fear being ourselves and being known.

Fear of rejection keeps us intent on "fitting in," rather than belonging.

Fitting in gets in the way of belonging.

Fitting in is about assessing a situation, and molding ourselves into who we think we must become in order to be accepted.

"Belonging, on the other hand, doesn't require us to change who we are; it requires us to be who we are" (Brené Brown, *The Gifts of Imperfection*, p. 25).

God now turns towards his beloved Eve, and asks her, *"What have you done?"*

Eve, now feeling small, afraid, rejected and shamed, answers, "The serpent seduced me. That's why I ate it."

Eve assumes she is rejected and has to change her story. She **excuses** her behavior by blaming the serpent for his seductive and deceitful behavior.

What's wrong with this?

Excuses, like blame, keep us from taking responsibility for our own actions.

Introspection is difficult but necessary.

Even when an issue is only 5% our part, we still have a piece to own.

In leading others, I've been challenged to ask, *"What is my part in the problem I'm complaining about right now?"*

When we don't make excuses but instead take responsibility, change happens and relationships can both grow and deepen.

CHECKLIST: Shame invites loss of vulnerability, fear and hiding, blame and rejection, **and excuses.**

I've tried to teach my children about real and productive apologies. "Apologies do not explain," I say. Even if it's an accident, to show real empathy and concern for the other, to seek reconciliation in the wrath of a wrong, we cannot start by excusing or explaining our own behavior.

Excuses give us permission to pass the buck. Often, the one we pass the buck to is someone we love the most.

Can't you just see Adam and Eve shifting miserably in their uncomfortable new clothes of fig leaves, seeking to cover the shame spiral of fear, hiding, rejection, blame and excuses?

Sadly, it only gets worse.

God tells the serpent, "You won't get away with this. Consequences always exist for life outside my boundaries."

Here's yours:

> "You may be the most shrewd of all the wild animals, but now you will **slink** along on your belly groveling in the dirt. And, this makes you **vulnerable** to your new enemy: women. Her offspring will strike your head and you will strike his heel."

Then, God turns toward Eve:

> "Having children is going to be a most **painful** experience. You will have **great desire** for your husband, but you will try to **control** him and he will **rule** over you."

CHECKLIST: Shame invites loss of vulnerability, fear and hiding, blame and rejection, excuses, **physical pain, control and unfulfilled desire.**

Oh, the tangled web we weave with our dance of control and domination, control and passivity.

Remember the hilarious movie, *"My Big Fat Greek Wedding?"*

Watch the video: *My Big Fat Greek Wedding.* Go to https://www.youtube.com/watch?v=Yel XdFhQxRQ&feature=youtu.be or scan the QR Code.

It revolved around a Greek family where a big show is made of the men's leadership within the family. However, the women proudly declare, "He may be the head, but the neck moves the head."

***Manipulation* and *control* are fruits of shame.**

Instead of relational oneness, mutual submission, and care for another that demands sacrifice of self, the Genesis consequences introduce a cycle of unhealthy manipulation and uncaring control.

When what we want seems out of reach, (like the fruit on the *Tree of the Knowledge of Good and Evil)*, we maneuver to get what we want, often by being manipulative. We delude ourselves, thinking instead about how much we *deserve it,* after all.

Our cultural belief, *"I deserve to be happy"* often gives us an excuse to stomp on those around us to get our way.

It gives us permission to forsake delayed gratification and to impulsively move toward instant satisfaction.

Are you still with me?

The growing checklist is so depressing, it seems like the best thing to do is to move on.

To move on is to skip the real work.

To be unaware is to be ignorant. And ignorance is not bliss.

Ignorance is a prison – one that keeps us from becoming everything our Creator desires for us. Instead, when we recognize what his happening in a situation, we should take steps to change it.

I envision Adam's loving Father looking deeply into his eyes, as tears run down his cheeks.

His father is devastated at the new reality for his heavenly garden, and the painful consequences for his beloved children.

> "Adam, I am sad to tell you that because you listened to your wife instead of protecting the garden, **(apathy),** your vocational work is going to be a **challenge**. It will cause you as much pain as your wife in childbirth. It will cause your body to hurt, obstacles will arise from every direction, it will seem as if you can never get ahead, **(hopelessness)** until one day your body will **die.**"

CHECKLIST: Shame invites loss of vulnerability, fear and hiding, blame and rejection, excuses, physical pain, control and unfulfilled desire, **apathy, vocational struggle, hopelessness and death.**

So, there we have it. The once heavenly garden has become a prison of shame.

Will they figure out the lies shame relentlessly tempts them to believe or will they fall into the abyss, never to find their way back out?

As we await the answer; let's turn our attention inward. Let's identify the lies shame speaks to each of us, tempting us to the same "fruitfulness" Adam and Eve experienced. As we identify the lies of shame, we can also rediscover the reality of *"being naked and knowing no shame."*

Reflect:

1. *Look back:* Where has shame entered into your story? Is there a history of shame in one part of your story? Is there currently a shame supplier from someone or some behavior?

2. *Take inventory:* What evidence of the shame spiral do you see in your life? Where is the list most descriptive of your relationships? Personal beliefs about yourself? Behaviors you exhibit? Are you taking responsibility or making excuses?

3. *Dream forward:* What would freedom from the shame spiral offer you?

DO Something:

See the **Appendix** on eradicating the lies shame tells us, and replacing them with truth. Begin a daily practice of speaking aloud the promises that speak to your own story. Eradicate the lies that you live with, and fill in the empty spot with the truth. Say the scriptures aloud.

This process is guaranteed to change your life in dramatic ways, setting you free for the life you were created to live. Your Creator knows "You were Meant for More!"

CHAPTER 7

EVICTION FROM THE GARDEN: JUDGMENT OR MERCY?

Adam and Eve were meant to live forever in the Garden of Eden. In reality, it was heaven on earth. As they ate from the *Tree of Life* they were given supernatural sustenance to increase life and never die.

With this reality in mind, consider the possibility of eternal life in the garden where evil now resides. We explored the downward spiral of shame's quick results, but consider the multiplied effects through time.

I used to believe God **judged** his children severely by evicting them from his garden. I thought he was harsh in withholding their rightful place in the garden.

I know better now.

Their father, in his **mercy,** acted to bring them an opportunity for life once again in the true garden: **heaven!**

Here's the deal: *if Adam and Eve continued to eat from the Tree of Life, they would live forever in the sin filled, evil exposed, Garden of Eden.*

They would never be set free to experience the shame-free life of innocence, purity and vulnerable transparency with their father and one another.

However, if they experience the painful reality of life outside the garden surrounded by evil, their bodies would eventually die, and they could be reunited with their heavenly father and one another, to live the shame-free heavenly life for which they were created.

This is what happened:

> God said, "Adam and Eve have become like us, knowing both good and evil. What if they reach out and take the fruit from the *Tree of Life* and eat it? Then they will live forever!"

God did not send Adam and Eve outside the garden uncovered, however. He made the sacrificial choice to introduce death into his garden designed for life: he killed one of the animals so that his beloved children would be clothed.

Even as I write this, I hurt for God.

> I can only imagine his despair as he took a knife to plunge into his creation, his good creation, to cause it to die.

It went against everything God wanted for his treasured creation.

I hear his scream as he does it.

Oh, the pain of lost dreams.

Oh, the pain and utter agony of death.

We know God abhors death, because he created us to live.

I Corinthians 15 tells us, "For Christ must reign until he humbles all his enemies beneath his feet. **And the last enemy to be destroyed is death.**"

Death is God's enemy.

*Think about it: your heavenly father loves you so much, he was willing to introduce his enemy into the world, **so you would LIVE!***

It was important for Adam and Eve to have physical clothes to cover their nakedness, but an even greater reason exists for spiritual clothes.

> Unless God had killed his creation, Adam and Eve would have been evicted from not only the garden but also from God's presence FOREVER!

> Blood needed to be shed so Adam and Eve could have the spiritual covering to continue relationship with God.

> Hebrews 9:22 tells us, "Without the shedding of blood, *there can be no forgiveness.*"

> God's ultimate purpose in killing his creation was to provide forgiveness and an ongoing pathway for relationship with himself and one another to continue.

Here's the most important part for us to realize:

> **When our loving, forgiving, merciful heavenly father took the knife and caused blood to flow in his creation, he knew he would be introducing death to his most beloved one, his son Jesus, as the final blood sacrifice.**

> Hebrews 10:10 states, "For God's will was for us to be made holy by the sacrifice of the body of Jesus Christ, once for all time."

Can you imagine a love this strong and pure?

You are so important to your heavenly father that he was willing to exchange his first son Jesus in death so you can live.

So the next time you hear the taunting lies of the slithering serpent, remember, remember, remember the truth, *you were meant to live!*

You are created to live—not a scratching-by existence, consumed by the downward spiral of shame, but to live, fully free, fully known, fully naked but knowing no shame.

Reflect:

1. *Look back:* What other experiences have you had with the Genesis story of Adam and Eve in the Garden? Do you remember exploring it as a child? In high school? If yes, did you see God as lovingly merciful or harshly judgmental? If this is your first exploration, did you react emotionally? Did you have questions?

2. *Take inventory:* What is the good news of the garden eviction in your own words? What is the application of Adam and Eve's expulsion to our story and life today?

3. *Dream forward:* Take 10 minutes to imagine life with a father who runs to give you a big bear hug the moment he sees you, listens to your every thought with great interest, recognizes your innate gifts and strengths, and provides the training and opportunity to live them out.

Do Something:

Look for ways around you that death leads to life. Think about nature and the rhythm of the lifecycle that continually creates life with death along the way.

CHAPTER 8

HEAVEN'S ANSWER TO SHAME

I f you don't believe shame is on God's mind, think again. Scripture contains **358** references to shame. Much of it is God moving to shame our enemies because of his great love for us. It's like the Dad who goes to defend his daughter on the playground because the bully has been taunting her and making her life miserable.

Shame is our enemy.

It taunts us and makes our life miserable. Our Dad moves on our behalf to put shame to death.

Absorb this Scripture in Psalm 34:4-6:

I prayed to the Lord, and he answered me.

He freed me from all my fears.

Those who look to him for help will be radiant with joy;

no shadow of SHAME will darken their faces.

In my desperation I prayed, and the Lord listened;

He saved me from all my troubles.

Isaiah 61 is one of my favorite chapters in the entire Bible. It is filled with so much hope, as God brings forth promises of his recompense in our lives. To recompense is to make restitution for all the theft, suffering, injury and harm we have experienced.

Isaiah 61:8 states, "For I, the Lord, love justice. I hate robbery and wrongdoing. I will faithfully recompense my people for their suffering and make an everlasting covenant with them." (link to True Purpose for covenant definition)

It's preceded by Is 61:7 which proclaims, "Instead of SHAME and dishonor, you will enjoy a double share of honor. You will possess a double portion of prosperity in your land, and everlasting joy will be yours!"

Pretty cool, isn't it? **Our God is actively replacing the shame and dishonor we've experienced with a restitution of a double share of honor, prosperity, and joy.**

How does this work? What makes it possible? We find the answer in Hebrews 12:1-2:

> Therefore, since we are surrounded by such a huge crowd of witnesses to the life of faith, *let us strip off every weight that slows us down*, especially the sin that so easily trips us up. And let us run with endurance the race God has set before us. We do this by keeping our eyes on Jesus, the champion who initiates and perfects our faith. Because of the joy awaiting him, he endured the cross, disregarding its SHAME. Now he is seated in the place of honor beside God's throne.

I trained for two marathons. At first, I would take a pack full of weighty items, but after a few long treks, I realized I needed to lighten my load. Shame weighs us down and makes our life incredibly challenging. It does this by drawing us back towards our old accusations – this leads us in circles, rather than to the finish line!

Jesus teaches us how to live a life of shame-free faith.

He invites us to lock eyes with him, as we watch him walk the road to immense suffering, wearing a sign which reads: "I am giving my life to be crucified as I exchange (your name)'s shame for my life of freedom and love."

Read Hebrews 12:1-2 again, out loud as you personalize it:

Therefore, since I am surrounded by such a huge crowd of witnesses to the life of faith, I choose to *strip off every weight that slows me down,* especially the sin that so easily trips me up. And I run with endurance the race God has set before me. I do this by keeping my eyes on Jesus, the champion who initiates and perfects our faith. *Because of the joy awaiting him, he endured the cross, disregarding its SHAME, for me.* Now he is seated in the place of honor beside God's throne.

Do you see how Jesus responded to his assignment to exchange his death for our shame-free life?

"Because of the joy awaiting him, he endured the cross, despising the shame."

Could it really be joy that awaited him as he was humiliated, beaten, betrayed by his friends, mocked by the religious officials and shamed by the crowd?

It was joy, because Jesus was able to see through to the other side: a life in the garden where we are naked and yet experience no shame.

If Jesus was willing to do this for you, *are you willing* to let go of shame and receive the forgiveness, freedom and peace Jesus died to give you?

Reflect:

1. *Look back:* What did you expect when you started this book? What was your attitude going into it? What did you hope you would experience by the end?

2. *Take inventory:* How are you feeling today? What emotions dominate your heart? What thoughts continually spin in your head? Are you playing a similar soundtrack with messages of shame and hiding as in previous days, or are you taking out that tape and finding a new song?

3. *Dream Forward:* What do you want to do now? With the changes you've made in your mind and in your heart, what will you do differently in your relationships with God, yourself, and your friends and family?

Do Something:

Finish well. You've walked a long and winding road through a garden. Take a break. Do something that is the opposite of feeling spun out, burned out, or overwhelmed. Find a way to connect to a calm that comes when you are free to be fully you, free to accept unconditional and healing love. This is unique to you. Block out a whole day, or at least a few hours, and do something restorative. You are out of the shame spiral. You are free to live—freely!

Watch video: *T.C. Ryan, Part 2,* https://www. youtube.com/watch?v=HEglUnK_8HU&feature=yo utu.be, or scan the QRCode.

Watch video: *Where do You Go From Here?* http://www.reclaimidentity.org/where-do-we-go-from-here1.html or scan the QRCode.

www.ReclaimIdentity.org

CHAPTER 9

WHERE DO YOU GO FROM HERE?

Life without shame: it's a vision worth pursuing. **It's the life we were created to live.**

Now that you understand this, what steps are you willing to take, in order to fight for the life you were meant to live?

We've identified and developed some tools to resource you for your journey out of being spun out by shame into reclaiming your sanity.

1. Engage the *Shame Stealers Replaced by Truth Sealers* on a daily basis. (Found in the Appendix, p. 61).
2. Spend five minutes a day imagining a life without shame. (Our brains go to the most compelling picture and begin to align with those life experiences.)

3. Read other e-books: *Green Embraces: Identity Reclaimed* is a great one to start next.

4. Read Tom Ryan's book, *Ashamed No More,* and consider hosting his seminar, *"Spiritual Wholeness in a Sexually Broken World"* in your community.

5. Attend a *Reclaim Identity Retreat* in beautiful Sonoma County, CA

No matter which pathway you choose to reclaim your sanity from the spiral of shame, know all of heaven is for you, and is continually working to bring about your best--a life of freedom, a life without shame!

Shame Stealers Replaced by Truth Sealers

Our brains go to the most compelling picture. When we begin to stake our lives on truth, our brain literally reshapes and creates new pathways, which allow us to literally believe the truth of our Creator, rather than the lie of shame.

The more you read these truth sealers, the quicker the shame stealers get kicked out – permanently! Speak them out loud. Your brain needs to hear the words spoken in order to build the new pathways to your life of shame-free living, the freedom Jesus died to impart to you. You are worth the investment!

❖ **Shame Stealer:**

Shame is part of me—I've always been this way:

You are made in God's image. You have his DNA and his characteristics. You look like he does! God created his world to live without shame. Shame is something that happened to you, not the core of who you are.

Truth Sealers:

Genesis 1:26a-27: "Let us make human beings in our image, make them reflecting our nature. God created human beings; he created them godlike, reflecting God's nature. He created them male and female.

Ephesians 2:10: For you are God's masterpiece, created to do good works which he designed long ago.

Psalm 139:13-14: Oh yes, you shaped me first inside, then out; you formed me in my mother's womb.

I thank you, High God—you're breathtaking!

Body and soul, I am marvelously made!

❖ Shame Stealer:

I am not good enough to be _____:

Our worth doesn't come from what we do, it comes from our heavenly father.

We are good enough because we are related to the Creator of the Universe who stated after his creation of humanity: God looked over all he had created and saw that it was very GOOD!

Serpents lie in saying that we don't deserve to receive our Father's blessings. However, our heavenly father chooses to give us good gifts because we are his children, not because we have done anything to earn it.

When Jesus became baptized, he heard the word of his father tell him, "You are my beloved son, in whom I take great delight." The interesting part of his identity affirmation is at that point of Jesus' life, he hadn't yet performed any miracles, or taught any great truths. He was an unknown carpenter in a small Jewish town.

It is the same for you.

Truth Sealers:

Mark 1:11: "You are my dearly loved child, and you bring me great joy." (This is our father's word to all his kids!)

1 John 3:1- "How great the love the father has lavished on us that we shall be called Children of God and that is what we are."

❖ **Shame Stealer:**

I don't deserve to be happy:

Happiness is a fleeting emotion that shifts like sand.

We were created to experience JOY, which is not dependent on circumstances or worthiness. It is a supernatural result of living life with God.

Truth Sealers:

Philippians 4:4,6-7: Always be full of joy in the Lord. I say it again—rejoice! Don't worry about anything; instead, pray about everything. Tell God what you need, and thank him for all he has done. Then you will experience God's peace, which exceeds anything we can understand. His peace will guard your hearts and minds as you live in Christ Jesus.

John 16:23-24: Jesus invites you: "I tell you the truth, you will ask the Father directly, and he will grant your request because you use my name. You haven't done this before. Ask, using my name, and you will receive, and *you will have abundant joy.*"

John 15:11: Jesus shares his joy: "I've told you these things for a purpose: **that my joy might be your joy,** and your joy wholly mature."

Hebrews 12:2: We do this by keeping our eyes on Jesus, the champion who initiates and perfects our faith. Because of the **joy** awaiting him, he endured the cross, disregarding its **shame.** Now he is seated at the place of honor besides God's throne.

❖ **Shame Stealer:**

If I do everything perfectly, I will be accepted:

Perfectionism is a prison from which we cannot escape.

Interestingly, the call to perfectionism even made it into the Bible but it came from a Greek word, *telios,* which also means "maturity."

How does this shift the scripture that says, "Be perfect as your heavenly father is perfect." (Matthew 5:48)

It becomes "Be mature as your heavenly father is mature."

Our heavenly father isn't a bit interested in perfectionism. He wants us to become mature adults, changing based on what we learn from making mistakes and healing along the way, not children continuing our destructive patterns.

Truth Sealers:

Matthew 5:48: "You are to be mature as your heavenly father is mature."

❖ **Shame Stealer:**

If I change who I am, people will like me better:

Our Creator created us to be like himself: each one of us has a unique purpose that only we can fulfill. If we move away from his design for us, we will constantly experience frustration and despair.

Shame is what moved Adam and Eve to run and hide. They were afraid of being judged or rejected, so they moved away from the heart of their father.

When we make an intentional decision to trust our heavenly father, to believe he created us for relationship and purpose, we experience freedom to like ourselves. When we like ourselves, others will appreciate us too!

Truth Sealers:

Psalm 139:13-14- "You made all the delicate, inner parts of my body and knit me together in my mother's womb.

Thank you for making me so wonderfully complex. Your workmanship is marvelous- how well I know it."

Ephesians 1:4, "Even before he made the world, God loved us and chose us in Christ to be holy and without fault in his eyes."

❖ **Shame Stealer:**

If I engage my addiction, it will make my shame go away:

We may experience momentary relief, but engaging anything which seeks to fill our "God-hole of desire" will ultimately increase shame—which results in the downward spiral of secrecy, silence and judgment.

The devil tempted Jesus to satisfy himself with bread in the desert. Jesus had the courage to say no to the temptation as he recognized, "we do not live by bread alone (or addiction) but by every word which proceeds from the mouth of God." God alone has the full ability to meet us in our "hunger," in whatever form this takes.

When we take the courageous step of turning toward God to "fill us," we are building trust. He loves us so much, he comes *running* to meet us in our desire.

Truth Sealers:

John 6:35: Jesus replied, "I am the bread of life. Whoever comes to me will never be hungry again. Whoever believes in me will never be thirsty."

Matthew 5:6: God blesses those who hunger and thirst for justice, for they will be satisfied.

❖ **Shame Stealer:**

Who am I to believe that I could _____?

Who are you to believe you can't? This point was driven home to me by the 2014 Super Bowl. The Denver Broncos played the Seattle Seahawks. Denver had the experienced quarterback Peyton Manning, but Seattle had a 26 year kid, Russell Wilson, who two years earlier was playing minor league baseball. But what Russell Wilson had was an attitude of invincibility, because he believed he could!

Read blog, *Why Not You?* Go to http://tamara-buchan.com/2015/01/why-not-you/ or scan the QR Code.

His dad built into Russell an identity and a sense of destiny in asking him the question, "Why can't it be you?" Even though Russell Wilson went to Peyton Manning's quarterback training camp as a teen, he believed in his ability to overcome the giants!

Wilson infected his team with the question, "Why not us?" And so, a team which was relatively inexperienced with few known stars came up against the "big gun." It turns out the big gun was no match for the belief that each one of us has a specific purpose in which God says to us, "_____, why not you?" I created you to follow me in overcoming all adversity and to live out God's dreams he deposited in us.

Truth Sealers:

Philippians 4:13: I have strength for all things in Christ Who empowers me [I am ready for anything and equal to anything through Him Who infuses inner strength into me.]

John 14:12: Jesus says, "I tell you the truth, anyone who believes in me will do the same works I have done, and even greater things because I am going to be with our Father."

See also: John 14:11-14 in the Message

❖ **Shame Stealer:**

Shame keeps me safe by wrapping itself around me like a warm blanket:

Shame is a prison, not a comfort. The warm blanket is more like a 10 foot by 10 foot walled prison—fortunately, Jesus has the keys to free you.

Truth Sealers:

John 8:31-32: Then Jesus turned to the people who had claimed to believe in him. "If you stick with this, living out what I tell you, you are my disciples for sure. Then you will experience for yourselves the truth, and the **truth will free you.**"

❖ **Shame Stealer:**

Shame is my friend:

Shame is both God's enemy and yours. Check out the shame checklist again, and consider how you have experienced the downward spiral in your own life. After that, ask yourself: is shame truly your friend?

Truth Sealers:

John 14:18: Jesus tells us, "I will not abandon you as orphans, I will come to you."

John 15:12-15: Jesus teaches us, "This is my command: Love one another the way I loved you. This is the very best way to love. Put your life on the line for your friends. You are my friends when you do the things I command you. I'm no longer calling you servants because servants don't understand what their master is thinking and planning. **No, I've named you friends because I've let you in on everything I've heard from the Father.**"

❖ **Shame Stealer:**

If I shame and blame others, I can be okay:

By shaming and blaming, Adam's life was wrecked: he became unemployed, separated from his heavenly father, lost intimacy and trust with his wife, and was evicted from the garden. He was definitely not okay after he shamed and blamed!

Truth Sealers:

I Thessalonians 5:23-24: "May God himself, the God of peace, sanctify you through and through. May your whole spirit, soul and body be kept blameless at the coming of our Lord Jesus Christ. The one who calls you **is faithful and he will do it!**"

Ephesians 1:3-5: "All praise to God, the Father of our Lord Jesus Christ, who has blessed us with every spiritual blessing in the heavenly realms because we are united with Christ. **Even before he made the world, God loved us and chose us in Christ to be holy and blameless in his sight.** God decided in advance to adopt us into his own family by bringing us to himself through Jesus Christ. This is what he wanted to do, and it gave him great pleasure."

❖ **Shame Stealer:**

If I shame and blame others, I don't have to carry the guilt:

Adam's downfall came from abdicating his role as protector of the garden. Shaming and blaming others only brings greater shame and its downward affects. Guilt may disappear momentarily, but it invites the entire shame spiral to increase.

Truth Sealers:

Read 2 Samuel 11-12. King David also abdicated his role by staying home from the war. He ended up falling for the temptation of a beautiful woman – a married beautiful woman. Driven crazy by temptation, David sent her husband to the front of the war efforts, where he was ultimately killed. David had the husband out of the way and was ready to move in on his desires.

God sent his prophet Nathan to confront David. Instead of blaming and shaming, David responded to the conviction and owned his sin. David wrote Psalm 51 as his confession.

❖ Shame Stealer:

I will be shamed if I am weak or show emotion:

Our greatest strength is to be able to be transparent and show vulnerability. Smothering our emotions and refusing to ask for help stunts our emotional growth, keeps us isolated and alone, and cuts off access to our soul.

Truth Sealers:

David was known as a man after God's own heart; he never held back from expressing emotion, some of it extreme. He teaches us much about life through the numerous Psalms he wrote. Take time to read some of the following Psalms, and observe the pattern of great emotion at the beginning, ending with a declaration of his faith and trust in God's ability to bring good out of painful circumstances.

Psalm 22, Psalm 28, Psalm 55, Psalm 69, Psalm 141, Psalm 142, Psalm 143

❖ Shame Stealer:

If I control my world, I can keep shame at bay:

Control comes from lack of trust. Eve fell prey to the lie that her father wasn't for her, didn't have her best at heart, and was holding out on her. She sought to control when she found her trust had been broken. When we trust our heavenly father, we can let go of control and live in freedom.

Philippians 3:20-21 states, "But our citizenship is in heaven. And we eagerly await a Savior from there, the Lord Jesus Christ, who, by the **power that enables him to bring everything under his control**, will transform our lowly bodies so that they will be like his glorious body."

Our process of maturing takes us through a journey of opportunity to relinquish control as we actively follow Jesus, who has the power to bring every situation under his control. As we do this, we are developing **self-control**; the **opposite** of control. **Control robs us of life, self-control gives us life!**

Truth Sealers:

Zechariah 1:11: They reported their findings to the Angel of God in the birch grove: "We have looked over the whole earth and all is well. Everything's under control."

2 Peter 1:5-7: For this very reason, make every effort to add to your faith goodness; and to goodness, knowledge; and to knowledge, self-control; and to self-control, perseverance; and to perseverance, godliness; and to godliness, mutual affection; and to mutual affection, love.

Titus 1:11-13: For the grace of God has appeared that offers salvation to all people. It teaches us to say "No" to ungodliness and worldly passions, and to live self-controlled, upright and godly lives in this present age, while we wait for the blessed hope—the appearing of the glory of our great God and Savior, Jesus Christ.

❖ Shame Stealer:

The world would be a better place if I weren't in it.

Jesus told us, "The thief comes to lie, steal and destroy, but I came home so you would have an abundant and fulfilling life." Have you ever considered that your life is so valuable and important to the world that you have been targeted by the thief to be lied to, stolen from and destroyed?

Truth Sealers:

Matthew 10:28-31: Don't be afraid of those who want to kill your body; they cannot touch your soul. What is the price of two sparrows—one copper coin? But not a single sparrow can fall to the ground without your Father knowing it. And the very hairs on your head are all numbered. So don't be afraid; **you are more valuable to God than a whole flock of sparrows.**

Spun Out on Shame Introduction

Shame.

We've all heard the expression, "Shame on You."

Perhaps we heard it daily growing up. Maybe it's left an indelible imprint upon us – so much so that no matter how many times we try to push it back into the dark corner of our mind, It Manages to Pop Out and Remind Us over and over, "You aren't Good Enough--you aren't worthy to be happy, to be loved, to succeed."

Maybe you've dealt with shame.

You want to be free.

Perhaps you've gone to counseling and gotten clear about why you experience shame and your head understands the "shame on you" messages don't belong.

But, does your heart know it too?

- Shame tries to tell us we don't belong; we were meant to feel alone and lonely.

- Shame lies to us, telling us we can't succeed; our dreams were meant to be buried and forgotten. forever.

- Shame wraps around us like armor, keeping us from experiencing friendship and intimacy with others, telling us over and over, it's better this way; then they will never know what a screw up we are.

73

Here's the reality for all of us.

Shame Steals.

It robbed the first people in the Garden of Eden, Adam and Eve, and it's robbed everyone ever created, including you. Including me. None of us have escaped it completely.

Shame Lies.

And, it's time to destroy it forever in our lives.

Come with me on this journey and together we can discover the root of our shame and dig It out, setting the landscape of our lives onto a solid foundation of identity as the beloved, unconditionally accepted, celebrated, kids of our creator: our Heavenly Father.

The "Naked" Truth

Have you ever heard people call the Bible boring?

There was a time when I thought the same. But, now I see that it has all the Bible has all the Elements of a Great Story. In some passages, the truth is provocative, other times, it's lying beneath the surface, waiting for us to stop, dig deeper and dive in.

Here's one example:

The second chapter of Genesis ends with the stunning declaration:

> "Adam and Eve were both naked and they felt no shame."

Interesting.

Adam and Eve were naked, and unashamed. What about us today? In my experience, there aren't many places I am naked and unashamed.

Think gym showers in awkward middle school years.

My birthday is in the middle of August so when I started junior high, I was barely 12. I was a really small child so when most of my friends began to develop, I was still flat chested. So board-like in fact, one embarrassing afternoon, my Mom took me to buy a bra, per my request to be like my friends, and the store couldn't find one small enough for me.

Consequently, I spent the whole summer before junior

high dreading gym class and the horrifying reality that I would have to be naked in front of my peers. I knew that my body didn't measure up. Despite the skin we see splattered on screens all around us, no one wants to be naked physically in Front of Unsafe People. For most of us, it's even worse to be naked emotionally.

How much energy do you spend trying to re-create and sustain your personality in order to make sure that no one knows the "Real You?"

Oppressively, doubt rattles around in our heads, "If they really knew _____ about me..., then they would._____ leave, laugh, abuse, exploit, discard, or avoid me."

How do you fill in the blanks??

Are you Wearing Emotional Clothes that Disguise the Real You?

Today we feel a connection between nakedness and shame.

In the garden, between Adam and Eve experienced emotional and spiritual nakedness. All this nakedness, and they didn't have any idea about shame. For Adam and Eve, Shame wasn't in their vocabulary—because shame didn't exist in their world.

It is the same world in which you were created to live. Shame. Leave it behind, You were Meant for More!

Where Do We Go From Here?

Life without shame. It's a vision worth pursuing.

It's the life we were created to live. Now that you understand this, what steps are you willing to take to fight for the life you were meant to live? We've identified and developed some tools to resource you for your journey out of being spun out by shame into reclaiming Your sanity:

1. Engage the Shame Stealers turned Life Sealers on a Daily Basis. (Found in the Appendix).

2. Spend Five Minutes a Day Imagining a Life without Shame. (Our brains go to the most compelling picture and begin to align with those life experiences.)

3. Read other e-books: Green Embraces: Identity Reclaimed is a great one to start next.

4. Read Tom Ryan's book *Ashamed No More,*and consider attending *"Spiritual Wholeness in a Sexually Broken World."*

5. Attend a *Reclaim Identity Retreat* in Beautiful Sonoma County, CA

No matter which pathway you choose to reclaim your sanity from the spiral of shame, know all of heaven is for you, and is continually working to bring about your best-- a Life of Freedom, a Life without Shame!

PREFACE

Spun Out on Shame Introduction
http://www.reclaimidentity.org/spun-out-on-shame-reclaim-your-sanity.html

Shame Stealer Replaced by Truth Sealers
http://www.reclaimidentity.org/shame-stealers.html

INTRODUCTION

Spun out on Shame Introduction
http://www.reclaimidentity.org/spun-out-on-shame-reclaim-your-sanity.html

CHAPTER I

"Let Her Go" by Passenger Band
https://www.youtube.com/watch?v=RBumgq5yVrA

CHAPTER 2

Identity Crisis: Reclaim the True You, Our Purpose, Chapter 1
http://www.reclaimidentity.org/chapter-1-our-true-purpose.html

Shared Life Relationships Reclaimed
http://www.reclaimidentity.org/a-shared-life-together-relationship-reclaimed.html

APPENDIX: VIDEOS

CHAPTER 3
The Naked Truth
http://www.reclaimidentity.org/the-naked-truth.
html

CHAPTER 5
Five Stages of Identity: Success Reclaimed
http://www.reclaimidentity.org/five-stages-of-
identity-success-reclaimed.html

T. C. Ryan, Part 1
https://www.youtube.com/watch?v=Ib8y2CGF3o
I&feature=youtu.be

T. C. Ryan, Part 2
https://www.youtube.com/watch?v=HEglUnK_
8HU&feature=youtu.be

CHAPTER 6
Brené Brown Ted Talks
https://www.ted.com/talks/
brene_brown_on_vulnerability

Brené Brown Ted Talks
http://embed.ted.com/talks/brene_brown_liste-
ning_to_shame.html

My Big Fat Greek Wedding
https://www.youtube.com/watch?v=YelXdFhQxR
Q&feature=youtu.be

APPENDIX: VIDEOS

CHAPTER 8
T.C Ryan, Part 2
http://www.reclaimidentity.org/where-do-we-go-from-here1.html

Where Do You Go From Here
http://www.reclaimidentity.org/where-do-we-go-from-here1.html

CHAPTER 9
Green Embraces: Identity Reclaimed
hhttp://www.reclaimidentity.org/green-embraces-identity-reclaimed.html

Reclaim Identity Retreats
http://www.reclaimidentity.org/retreats.html

APPENDIX
Shame Stealers Replaced by Truth Sealers
http://www.reclaimidentity.org/shame-stealers.html

Tamara J. Buchan is founder of Reclaim Ministries, ordained Evangelical Covenant pastor, Master of Divinity from Denver Seminary, speaker and author. However, these worldly credentials do not fulfill or thrill her nearly as much as her identity as beloved child and royal heir to her Heavenly Father. Tamara is passionate about her marriage to Bill, their adult daughters: Heather, Bonnie and Molly, and son-in-law Luke. Tamara and Bill reside in Sonoma County, California. Contact Tamara at tamarabuchan@gmail.com or visit www.ReclaimIdentity.org for information about "Reclaim Identity Retreats" in Sonoma County and availability to speak at your church or organization.

Lindsey D. Osborne is a freelance writer with a Masters of Divinity from Central Baptist Theological Seminary. She works as a Regional Trainer for Young Life and as a coach at a Crossfit affiliate. She and her husband and their three children live in Kansas City with family, grace, and adventure as hallmarks of their days and ways.

www.ReclaimIdentity.org

"YOU WERE MEANT FOR MORE" SERIES

Green Embraces: Identity Reclaimed
Book I

A strong handshake, a tender hug, a long embrace...being held feels good. As human beings built for connection, embraces carry power when they come from someone who knows us fully and loves us anyways. The embrace of God's powerfully loving arms began in a green garden long ago. The original design was a clean, lively, and green creation to host and hold people as they were meant to be. To lived loved was the original design. We've wandered and gotten lost, lived for less, and walked a winding road. However, the fresh, pure, living embrace of God who knows us as Beloved Child, is available to each of us, right now. It's up to us to reclaim what was ours all along.

Discover that we are truly loved, that our story is part of a greater divine story, that we are forgiven and truly accepted and that we have a true place of belonging. If embraced, these words have the power to bring true freedom, the kind of freedom that can only come when we see ourselves the way that God sees us, a beloved child of the King!

Available in paperback book and eBook

Identity Crisis: Reclaim the True You

What does a dried dandelion have to do with an identity crisis? Everything, if we stop looking at it from a gardener's perspective and start to understand its hidden value. The identities we adopt from the world are like dandelions the gardener fervently attacks before they dry up into the perfect ball of seeds, which spread all over the yard when the wind begins to blow. If we think about our enemy, the Devil, as the gardener, we begin to understand his motive is to convince us that our identities are worthless weeds: throwaways when compared to the beautiful rose bushes right next to us. Our enemy, the gardener, thrives when we agree that our identities are discarded weeds, rather than boldly reclaiming our true identities from our Master Gardener: the Creator of the Universe. To reclaim is to take that which is worthless and make it beautiful and productive again. An overgrown garden with dried dandelions can appear to be worthless. However, when the Master Gardener begins to blow the seeds, our lives suddenly "wake up" and start to take root in gardens we never dreamed we could inhabit.

Available in paperback book and eBook

"QUIET TIMES FOR THE HEART" SERIES

Seeking the Christmas Lamb
A Family Advent Handbook Forty Days of Celebrating Christ's Sacrifice Through the Season: Book 1

Is your Christmas more "Santa" than "Savior"? For many, the Christmas season has become synonymous with long lines at the department store and shiny wrapping paper. And in addition to presents under the tree and eggnog, there's something about a Savior born in a manger, right? *Seeking the Christmas Lamb* is a tool for the family who wishes to slow down and find the real reason to celebrate the holidays. Borrowing from her own quest for a meaningful celebration of Advent, author Tamara J. Buchan creates a journey through the twenty-eight days leading to Christmas and the twelve days of Epiphany. Rich but simple daily readings trace God's plan for humanity, from Genesis to Revelation, pivoting on the sacrificial Advent of His Son. Through these pages, you and your family can passionately pursue an intimate understanding of the season's significance. Discover how the Christmas season can help you find a new appreciation for Christ's Advent in your own life!

Available in eBook

Thank you for reading *Spun Out on Shame? Reclaim Your Sanity.* This is our second book of the 12- Book Series, *You were Meant for More.* The 12-Book Series is targeted for college students and young adults 20+, generated from our flagship book, *Identity Crisis: Reclaim the True You.*

Join us for our monthly Reclaim Ministry Interactive Conference calls, a platform hosting special guests, updates, support and encouragement. Bring your questions, testimonies and prayers as we share key insights, personal testimonies, and pray together. There will a Q & A Session at the end of each session allowing you time to ask your questions. Join us! If interested, contact us at www.ReclaimIdentity.org/contact.html and we will email you the conference call phone number/code, time zone to connect together. Invite a friend!

Explore our social media links and receive additional devotional tips, resources, and recipes for Reclaiming your Identity, Dreams and Destiny.

RECLAIM
MINISTRIES

www.ReclaimIdentity.org

Connect With Us

Follow me on Twitter:
https://twitter.com/tamarabuchan

Friend me on Facebook:
https:www.facebook.com/tamarajbuchan

Subscribe to my Blog:
http://tamarabuchan.com/blog/

View profile on LinkedIn:
https://www.linkedin.com/pubtamara-buchan/4/564/762

Follow me on Vimeo:
https://twitter.com/tamarabuchan

Follow me on YouTube:
https://www.youtube.com/user/TamaraBuchan

Favorite us at Smashwords:
https://www.smashwords.com/profile/view/tamarabuchan-
https://www.smashwords.com/profile/view/lindseyosborne

Email us if you are interested in joining our Reclaim Ministries monthly conference calls:
http://www.ReclaimIdentity.org

Learn about our Identity Retreats:
http://www.ReclaimIdentity.org/contact.html

41479310R00051

Made in the USA
Charleston, SC
29 April 2015